ALTARS *of* YEARNING

ALTARS *of* YEARNING

HOW INDIA PRAYS

SHRIPRIYA DALMIA THIRANI

RUPA

Published by
Rupa Publications India Pvt. Ltd 2018
7/16, Ansari Road, Daryaganj
New Delhi 110002

Sales centres:
Allahabad Bengaluru Chennai
Hyderabad Jaipur Kathmandu
Kolkata Mumbai

Grateful acknowledgement is made to all the photographers including Raj Sarkar, Nilayan Chatterjee, Rana Pandey, Kounteya Sinha, Debmalya Das, Ritesh Ghosh, Arpan Ganguly and Kallol Bhattacharjee for their help in making the book.

Book design: Bena Sareen

ISBN: 978-93-5333-280-8

10 9 8 7 6 5 4 3 2 1

Printed at Lustra Print Process Pvt. Ltd.

UCO BA
24 hour e-Lobby

INTRODUCTION

Have you ever wondered what makes India a superpower?
Many would say it's the country's nuclear arsenal while others would vouch for its armed forces.
But for me, India's real strength is in its people.
The world's largest democracy is a rich tapestry of multiple socio-cultural identities woven into a perfect single nation. It is in the idea of secularity and the freedom to worship that India finds its core strength–the theory of one in all and all in one.

Prayer for me is the greatest institution of human life much like language.
From one welcomed by birth or bid goodbye through death–prayer stays constant.
Through this book, I want to remind the world of India's incredible social fabric—a land of many people, many cultures and many religions coexisting peacefully as one—prayer being a common phenomenon among them.The moment we pray is when we are most real, most true, most vulnerable, most spontaneous and above all, most private.

India is a very large country. Documenting how it prays across this massive land mass is a real challenge. I have tried to document the institution of prayer from almost all its parts. The format that I followed was actually the lack of it—walked around aimlessly across the country and saw how it prayed. This approach intended to catch people unawares, at their private time.

Prayer for me is the greatest art form—expressing the inner yearning of the human soul—the moment when man in flesh connects to God in spirit. I greatly believe in the power of prayer. I prayed when I became a mother, I prayed when I became an entrepreneur and I pray almost every day. Don't ever make the mistake of thinking that prayer is a religious duty. It isn't about reciting religious texts nor is it about building expectations. Prayer for me is neither a mere mental exercise, nor a vocal performance. It is a spiritual state of unity between the soul and the spirit—a long winding pathway to find our true selves. Because it is in what we ask during a prayer that truly defines who we are.

~

'In prayer, all are equal'

\- Rumi

The moment we pray is when we are most real, most true, most vulnerable, most spontaneous and above all, most private. Prayer for me is neither a mere mental exercise, nor a vocal performance. It is a spiritual state of unity between the soul and the spirit—a long winding pathway to find our true selves. Because it is in what we ask during a prayer that truly defines who we are.

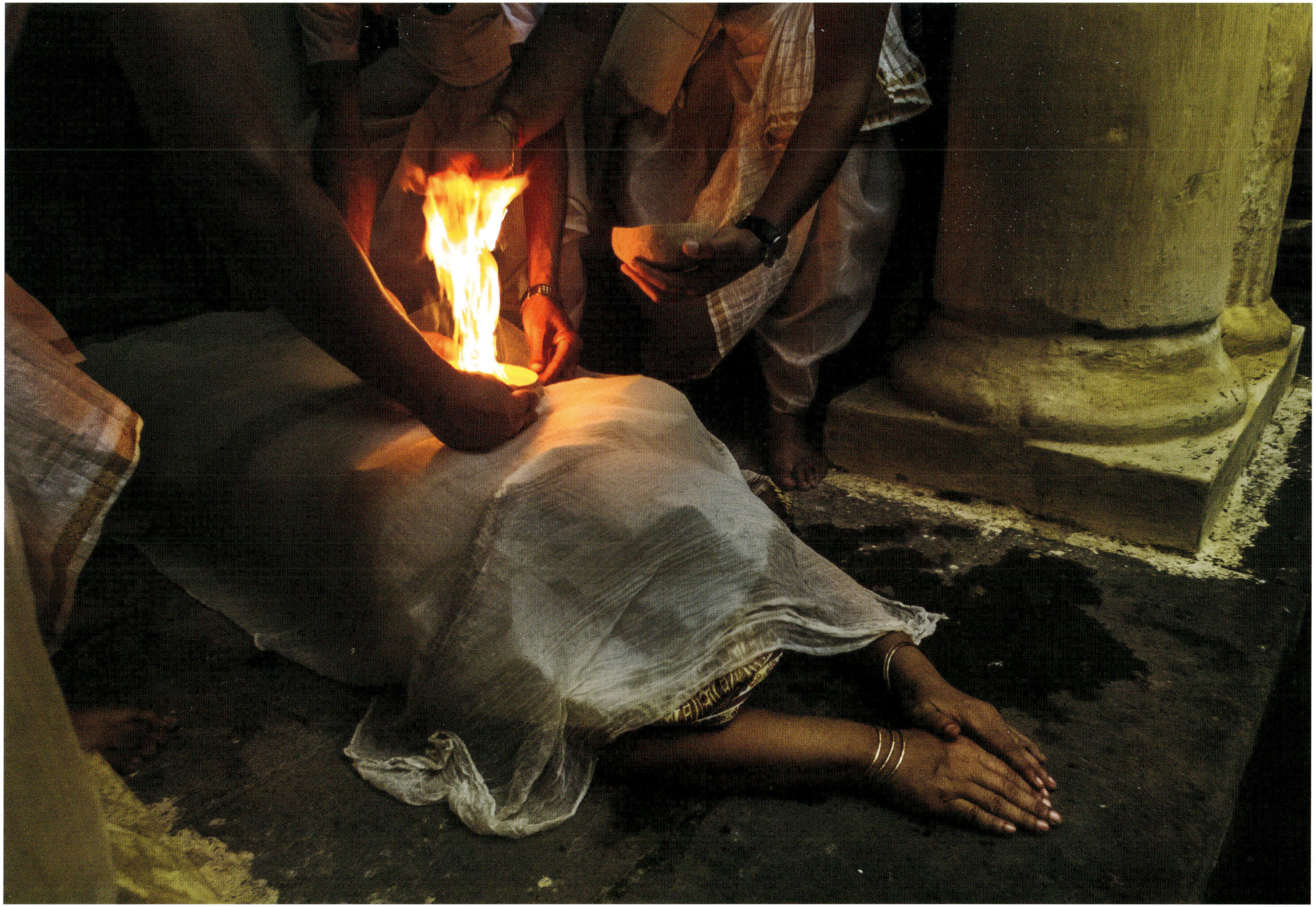

'Let me not pray to be sheltered from dangers,
But to be fearless in facing them.
Let me not beg for the stilling of my pain,
But for the heart to conquer it.
Let me not crave in anxious fear to be saved,
But for the patience to win my freedom.'
- Rabindranath Tagore

'Pray for knowledge and light; every other prayer is selfish.'
- Swami Vivekananda

'Prayer is not an old woman's idle amusement.
Properly understood and applied, it is the most
potent instrument of action.'

- Mahatma Gandhi

Prayer for me is the greatest art form—expressing the inner yearning of the human soul—the moment when man in flesh connects to God in spirit.

HISTORY OF
PART-III

*'You pray in your distress and in your need;
would that you might pray also in the fullness of your
joy and in your days of abundance.'*

\- Kahlil Gibran

Prayer for me is neither a mere mental exercise, nor a vocal performance. It is a spiritual state of unity between the soul and the spirit—a long winding pathway to find our true selves. Because it is in what we ask during prayer that truly defines who we are.

THE MIGHTY GOD

airtel
airtel
airtel
airtel
Coca-Cola

'Prayer is not asking. It is a longing of the soul. It is daily admission of one's weakness. It is better in prayer to have a heart without words than words without a heart.'

- Mahatma Gandhi

. 72 .

Because it is in what we ask during prayer that truly defines who we are.

महाआरती

107

'God speaks in the silence of the heart.
Listening is the beginning of prayer.'
- Mother Teresa

ORIGINAL

गुप्तदान गुप्त दान

. 96 .

'God, our creator, has stored within our minds and personalities, great potential strength and ability. Prayer helps us tap and develop these powers.'

- Dr A. P. J. Abdul Kalam

THE BENGAL TANNERY CO.
DEALERS OF QUALITY

A. R. Techno Pack Industries Pvt. Ltd
Regd. Office : 9B Dinabandhu Lane, Kolkata - 700 006
E-mail : technopack99@yahoo.co.in / technopack4@gmail.com
MAY 2018
SUN MON TUE WED THU FRI SAT

karROX

মানুষের যখন
কোনও অন্তর্দৃষ্টি
থাকে না
তখনই সে
বাহ্যিক
আয়োজন
শ্রীশ্রী

. 110 .

ନବକଳେବର ଉପଲକ୍ଷେ
ଭକ୍ତମାନଙ୍କ ସ୍ୱାଗତ ପାଇଁ
ଶ୍ରୀକ୍ଷେତ୍ର ପ୍ରସ୍ତୁତ
ଆଶ୍ରୟ ଲଜ୍
ASHRAYA LODGE
idea
relaxwell
HOTEL

TMC

ঘরের আলো

தீ

'I bow at His Feet constantly, and pray to Him, the Guru,
the true Guru, has shown me the way.'
- Guru Nanak

भिक्खु ज्ञानज्योती महाथेरो एवं भिक्खु संघ,
संघारामगिरी
पो.- बोथली त. चिमूर,
(महाराष्ट्र)
मनुष्य एवं अन्य

कृपया अपने सामान की सुरक्षा स्वंय करें।
अर्चिता
मंदिर परिसर में सफाई बनायें रखें।
अर्चिता
हे मेरे नाथ, मै आपको भूलू नहीं।
अर्चिता
मंदिर परिसर में सफाई बनायें रखें।
अर्चिता

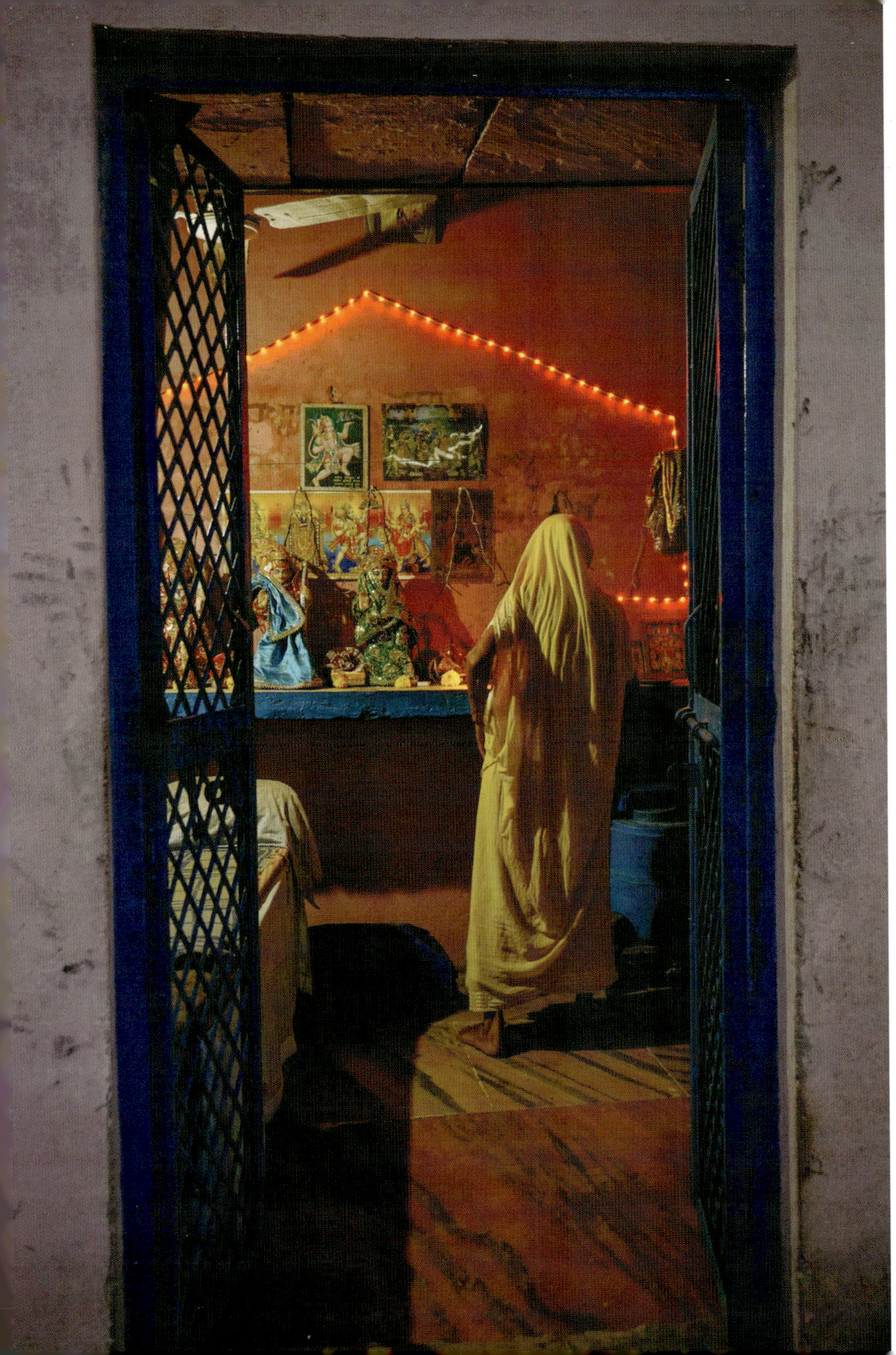

உலகளந்த பெருமாள் என அவர் எதிரிலேயே
மிகவும் தொன்மை வாய்ந்த இப்புண்ணிய தலத்தில்
அபிராமேசுவரர் ஆலயம் என்னும் இத்திருக்கோயில் உலகளந்த
தெருவில் சங்குபாணி விநாயகருக்கு வலப்பக்கத்தில் கிழக்கு
விளங்குகின்றது.
காஞ்சிப்புராணம் - அபிராமேசப்பட
புலவர் மா.வேங்கடேசன்.M.A.

ஓம் ஸ்ரீ சித்ரகுப்தாய நம: